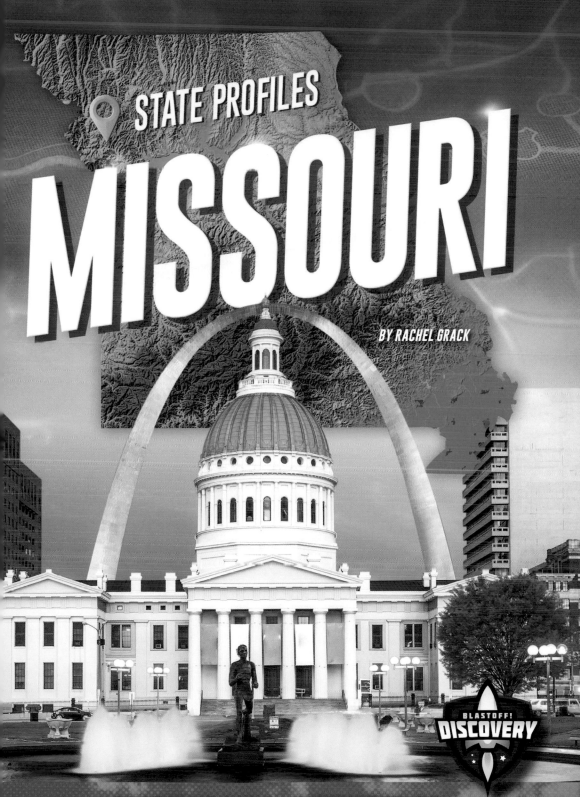

STATE PROFILES

MISSOURI

BY RACHEL GRACK

BELLWETHER MEDIA • MINNEAPOLIS, MN

Blastoff! Discovery launches a new mission: reading to learn. Filled with facts and features, each book offers you an exciting new world to explore!

BLASTOFF! UNIVERSE

BLASTOFF! Beginners

BLASTOFF! READERS

BLASTOFF! DISCOVERY

GRADE K

GRADES 1-3

GRADE 4

This edition first published in 2022 by Bellwether Media, Inc.

No part of this publication may be reproduced in whole or in part without written permission of the publisher.
For information regarding permission, write to Bellwether Media, Inc., Attention: Permissions Department,
6012 Blue Circle Drive, Minnetonka, MN 55343.

Library of Congress Cataloging-in-Publication Data

Names: Koestler-Grack, Rachel A., 1973- author.
Title: Missouri / by Rachel Grack.
Description: Minneapolis, MN : Bellwether Media, Inc., 2022. |
    Series: Blastoff! Discovery: State profiles | Includes bibliographical
    references and index. | Audience: Ages 7-13 | Audience: Grades
    4-6 | Summary: "Engaging images accompany information about
    Missouri. The combination of high-interest subject matter and
    narrative text is intended for students in grades 3 through 8"–
    Provided by publisher.
Identifiers: LCCN 2021019665 (print) | LCCN 2021019666 (ebook)
    | ISBN 9781644873304 (library binding) |
    ISBN 9781648341731 (ebook)
Subjects: LCSH: Missouri–Juvenile literature.
Classification: LCC F466.3 .K64 2022 (print) | LCC F466.3 (ebook)
    | DDC 977.8–dc23
LC record available at https://lccn.loc.gov/2021019665
LC ebook record available at https://lccn.loc.gov/2021019666

Editor: Betsy Rathburn   Designer: Andrea Schneider

Printed in the United States of America, North Mankato, MN.

TABLE OF CONTENTS

GATEWAY ARCH
ST. LOUIS

On a summer day, a family explores Gateway Arch National Park. First, they hike a trail along the Mississippi River. Then, they head inside the park's museum to explore fun history displays. One lets them pretend to be fur traders on the Mississippi River!

HA HA TONKA STATE PARK

LAKE OF THE OZARKS

ONONDAGA CAVE STATE PARK

SILVER DOLLAR CITY

When they are done exploring, the family boards a tram. They ride to the top of the 630-foot-tall (192-meter-tall) Gateway Arch. When the tram opens, they rush to the windows lining the hallway. One side shows a view of the Mississippi River far below. The other side shows the busy city of St. Louis. Welcome to Missouri!

WHERE IS MISSOURI?

Missouri is part of the **Midwestern** United States. Covering 69,707 square miles (180,540 square kilometers), it is the 21st largest state. Missouri shares its northern border with Iowa. The Mississippi River lines Missouri's eastern border. Across the river are Illinois, Kentucky, and Tennessee. Arkansas is to the south. Oklahoma, Kansas, and Nebraska share Missouri's western border.

The Missouri River passes many of Missouri's most important cities. It flows from Kansas City in the west towards Columbia, one of Missouri's largest cities. The river then flows south to Jefferson City, the state capital. It winds north of St. Louis before joining the Mississippi River.

NEBRASKA

KANSAS CITY

KANSAS

OKLAHOMA

IOWA

MISSISSIPPI
RIVER

ILLINOIS

MISSOURI
RIVER

COLUMBIA

ST. LOUIS

JEFFERSON CITY

MISSOURI

SPRINGFIELD

KENTUCKY —

TENNESSEE —

ARKANSAS

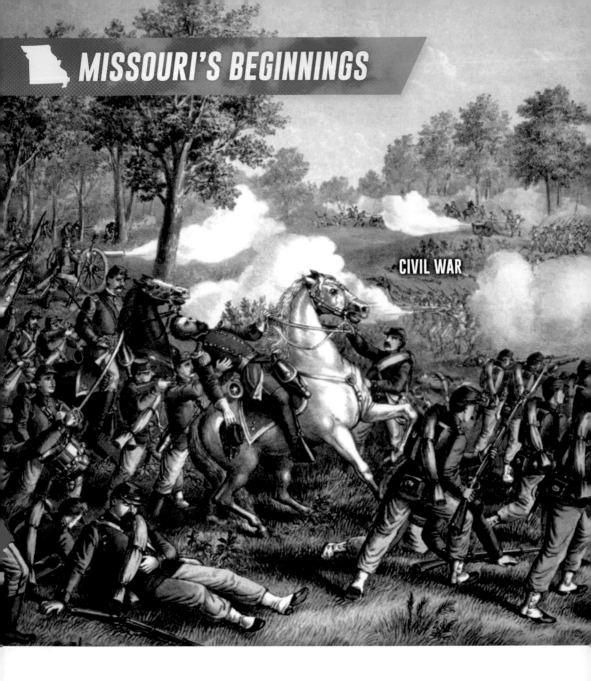

CIVIL WAR

People have lived in Missouri for at least 12,000 years. Among them were the Missouria, Osage, and Ioway people. In time, European **settlers** pushed other tribes into the area. They included the Shawnee, Delaware, and Kickapoo.

In the 1700s, French miners founded Sainte Genevieve. This became the first permanent European settlement in Missouri. In 1803, the United States bought Missouri from France in the **Louisiana Purchase**. Missouri became the 24th state in 1821. As part of the **Missouri Compromise**, slavery was allowed in the state. This led to a divided state during the **Civil War**.

NATIVE PEOPLES OF MISSOURI

Most Native Americans were forced to leave Missouri in 1830 due to the Indian Removal Act. There are no federally recognized tribes in the state today.

IOWAY

- Original lands in Minnesota, Iowa, and Missouri
- Descendants in the Iowa Tribe of Oklahoma and the Iowa Tribe of Kansas and Nebraska today
- Also called Iowa

ILLINOIS CONFEDERATION

- Original lands in Wisconsin, Iowa, Illinois, and Missouri
- Made up of around 12 tribes
- Also called Illini and Illiniwek

OTOE-MISSOURIA

- Original lands in the Great Lakes region and northern Missouri
- Formed from the Otoe people and Missouria people
- Descendants largely in Oklahoma
- Also called Jiwere (Otoe) and Nutachi (Missouria)

Plains cover much of Missouri. In the north, they are made up of rolling hills and slow streams. Much of the land is used for farming. Western Missouri is home to the flat Osage Plains. The Missouri River runs through central Missouri, meeting the Mississippi River in the east. In southern Missouri,

MISSISSIPPI RIVER

MISSOURI RIVER

N
W + E
S

OSAGE PLAINS   OZARK MOUNTAINS

the Ozark Mountains rise over the land. There are many caves, lakes, and springs in this region. Missouri's southeastern corner is covered in rich farmland.

OZARK MOUNTAINS

SPRING
HIGH: 66°F (19°C)
LOW: 44°F (7°C)

SUMMER
HIGH: 88°F (31°C)
LOW: 66°F (19°C)

FALL
HIGH: 68°F (20°C)
LOW: 46°F (8°C)

WINTER
HIGH: 42°F (6°C)
LOW: 23°F (-5°C)

°F = degrees Fahrenheit
°C = degrees Celsius

MISSOURI'S FUTURE: CLIMATE CHANGE

Missouri's climate is changing. Rising temperatures have caused heavier rainfall and greater flooding in the spring. Summers bring extreme heat and severe droughts. Over time, these conditions will affect farmland and corn harvests.

Missouri has hot summers and cold winters. Spring and summer can bring powerful tornadoes. In the mountains, the weather is more mild. Winters are warmer, and summers are cooler.

11

Across Missouri, coyotes and bobcats slink through tall grasses on the hunt for deer. Foxes and badgers prowl for mice, voles, and other rodents. Muskrats and otters scurry near rivers and streams. In the trees, goldfinches and blue jays perch on high branches. Snakes, salamanders, skinks, and toads hide in the brush below.

In Missouri's Ozark Mountains, black bears roam the forests. Bats hang in dark caves. Armadillos dig homes underground. Missouri's southeastern corner is home to alligator snapping turtles and broad-banded water snakes. Swamp rabbits also live in the region. This is the only place within the state that they are found!

NORTH AMERICAN RIVER OTTER

BARN OWL

GREAT PLAINS SKINK

ALLIGATOR SNAPPING TURTLE

NINE-BANDED ARMADILLO

SWAMP RABBIT

Life Span: around 2 years
Status: least concern

swamp rabbit range =

LEAST CONCERN	NEAR THREATENED	VULNERABLE	ENDANGERED	CRITICALLY ENDANGERED	EXTINCT IN THE WILD	EXTINCT

More than 6 million people live in Missouri. Most live in **urban** areas. The largest cities are Kansas City, St. Louis, and Springfield. Some Missourians live in small towns.

MISSOURI'S FUTURE: HEALTH CARE

Many Missourians who live far from cities have limited access to health care. Some live with health problems that could be treated. Finding ways to provide care for all Missourians would help people and businesses.

ST. LOUIS

GERMANY IN MISSOURI

Many early settlers near St. Louis came from Germany. Because of this, the area is sometimes called the Missouri Rhineland after the Rhineland region of Germany.

FAMOUS MISSOURIAN

Name: Becky Sauerbrunn

Born: June 6, 1985

Hometown: St. Louis, Missouri

Famous For: Professional soccer player for Portland Thorns FC, captain of the U.S. Women's National Soccer Team, Olympic gold medalist, and World Cup champion

Most Missourians are of European **descent**. About 1 out of 10 Missourians are African American or Black. Smaller numbers of Hispanic and Asian American people live in Missouri. Fewer than 1 out of 100 people in Missouri have Native American descent. The state has also welcomed many **immigrants**. Newcomers are from Mexico, China, India, and Vietnam.

Kansas City was first settled in 1821. It grew into a key river port. In the 1860s, an important railroad extended through Kansas City. The city became a major **manufacturing** and shipping center.

UNION STATION

Today, Kansas City is still a transportation **hub**. It is also a **cultural** center. People explore the city's musical history through exhibits and performances at the American Jazz Museum. Visitors shop and dine out in the historic River Market neighborhood. City Market is a popular shopping center. Shoppers buy fresh flowers, fruit, and meat at its huge farmer's market!

AMERICAN JAZZ MUSEUM

CITY MARKET
RIVER MARKET NEIGHBORHOOD

In its early days, Missouri's most important industry was farming. Cotton was one of the biggest crops. Today, soybeans and corn are important. Throughout the 1900s, manufacturing grew. Today, factories make trucks, aircraft, processed foods, and chemicals. Missouri is also rich with **natural resources**. Lead and zinc are mined in the southeast. Limestone is also important.

Most Missourians hold **service jobs**. Many people work in banking, especially in Kansas City and St. Louis. Others work in stores, restaurants, hospitals, and government buildings. Transportation jobs are also important. Missouri's rivers, railroads, and highways connect the state to many other places!

INVENTED IN MISSOURI

FIRST PUBLIC KINDERGARTEN IN THE U.S.

Date Invented: 1873

Inventor: Susan Elizabeth Blow

PANCAKE MIX

Date Invented: 1889

Inventors: Chris Rutt and Charles Underwood

7UP

Date Invented: 1929

Inventor: Charles Leiper Grigg

MONSTER TRUCKS

Date Invented: 1975

Inventor: Bob Chandler

BURNT ENDS

BBQ CITY

Kansas City has more than 100 barbecue restaurants!

Missouri is famous for barbecue! Burnt ends are a favorite dish. These smoky chunks of beef brisket are covered in thick barbecue sauce. They are often served on sandwiches or with beans. Gioia Deli in St. Louis is known for its hot salami sandwiches. They feature salami topped with chili peppers, onion, and spicy mustard. St. Louis-style pizza uses provel, a processed cheese invented in the city.

Ozark pudding is a favorite Missouri dessert. It is a thick **custard** made with fruit and nuts. Gooey butter cake is another popular Missouri sweet. Squares of this heavy, flat cake are dusted with powdered sugar just before serving.

ST. LOUIS-STYLE PIZZA

BUTTER CAKE

OZARK PUDDING

8
SERVINGS

Have an adult help you make this recipe.

INGREDIENTS

1 egg

3/4 cup sugar

2 tablespoons flour

1 1/4 teaspoon baking powder

1/4 teaspoon salt

1/2 cup chopped nuts

1/2 cup chopped apples

1 teaspoon vanilla

DIRECTIONS

1. Preheat oven to 350 degrees Fahrenheit (177 degrees Celsius).

2. In a large bowl, beat egg and sugar until smooth. Stir in flour, baking powder, and salt. Add nuts, apples, and vanilla.

3. Pour batter into a greased pie tin. Bake for 35 minutes.

4. Cool, then serve with whipped cream or ice cream.

KANSAS CITY
ROYALS

Missourians love sports! Football fans root for the
Kansas City Chiefs. The Kansas City Royals and St. Louis
Cardinals baseball teams are popular. Soccer fans
cheer for Sporting Kansas City. St. Louis Blues hockey
games draw big crowds!

Many Missourians vacation in Branson. The city hosts many concerts and other shows. Trips to the Gateway Arch in St. Louis are also popular. The Kauffman Center for the Performing Arts in Kansas City hosts ballets, operas, and symphony music. The Ozark Mountains offer plenty of outdoor fun. People enjoy camping, fishing, hiking, and exploring caves.

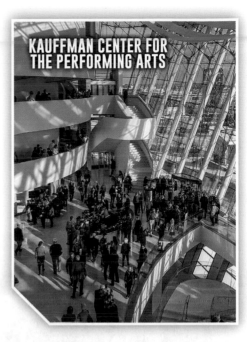

KAUFFMAN CENTER FOR THE PERFORMING ARTS

NOTABLE SPORTS TEAM

St. Louis Blues
Sport: National Hockey League
Started: 1967
Place of Play: Enterprise Center

Each spring, the Twain on Main festival in Hannibal honors the life of Missouri author Mark Twain. People gather to see magicians, listen to storytellers, and play games. People honor Irish culture, music, and dance at the Missouri River Irish Festival in St. Charles every May. May also brings the St. Louis African Arts Festival. The event features concerts, food, and art!

MISSOURI RIVER
IRISH FESTIVAL
ST. CHARLES

GARDEN GLOW

In the winter, many families visit Garden Glow at the Missouri Botanical Garden in St. Louis. They sip hot chocolate and roast marshmallows while surrounded by over 1 million twinkling lights!

Summer brings the Water Lantern Festival to Kansas City. People decorate paper lanterns and place lights in them. When it gets dark, they float the glowing lanterns in water. In the fall, the Roots N Blues Festival draws crowds to Columbia. Visitors listen to blues music and eat barbecue. There is plenty to celebrate in Missouri!

WATER LANTERN FESTIVAL

1808

A treaty with the U.S. government causes the Osage people to lose their land in Missouri

1700s

French miners found Sainte Genevieve

1821

Missouri becomes the 24th state

1804

Lewis and Clark depart from St. Louis to explore the land gained in the 1803 Louisiana Purchase

1820

The Missouri Compromise allows Missouri to join the country as a slave state, while Maine joins as a free state

1854 TO 1859

Groups in Kansas and Missouri fight over whether or not Kansas will become a slave state in an event called Bleeding Kansas

2020

Cori Bush is the first African American woman from Missouri elected to Congress

2011

A powerful tornado brings destruction to the city of Joplin

2006

Claire McCaskill is the first woman to be elected to the U.S. Senate from Missouri

1838

The Cherokee people pass through Missouri on the Trail of Tears

2014

The death of Michael Brown leads to nationwide protests against police brutality and racism

27

MISSOURI FACTS

Nickname: Show-Me State

Motto: *Salus Populi Suprema Lex Esto*
(Let the Welfare of the People Be the Supreme Law.)

Date of Statehood: August 10, 1821 (the 24th state)

Capital City: Jefferson City ★

Other Major Cities: Kansas City, St. Louis, Springfield, Columbia

Area: 69,707 (180,540 square kilometers); Missouri is the 21st largest state.

Population

6,154,913
(2020)

STATE FLAG

Missouri's flag is divided into three equal stripes. The top stripe is red for bravery. The middle stripe is white for purity. The bottom blue stripe represents justice. The state seal is in the center of the white stripe. It shows two bears standing on a gold scroll that contains the state motto. Below the scroll are Roman numerals showing Missouri's date of statehood. The bears hold a shield that reads "United We Stand Divided We Fall" around the sides. In the center of the shield is a crescent moon, a bear, and the Great Seal of the United States. Above the shield is a gold helmet with 24 stars above it.

INDUSTRY

Main Exports

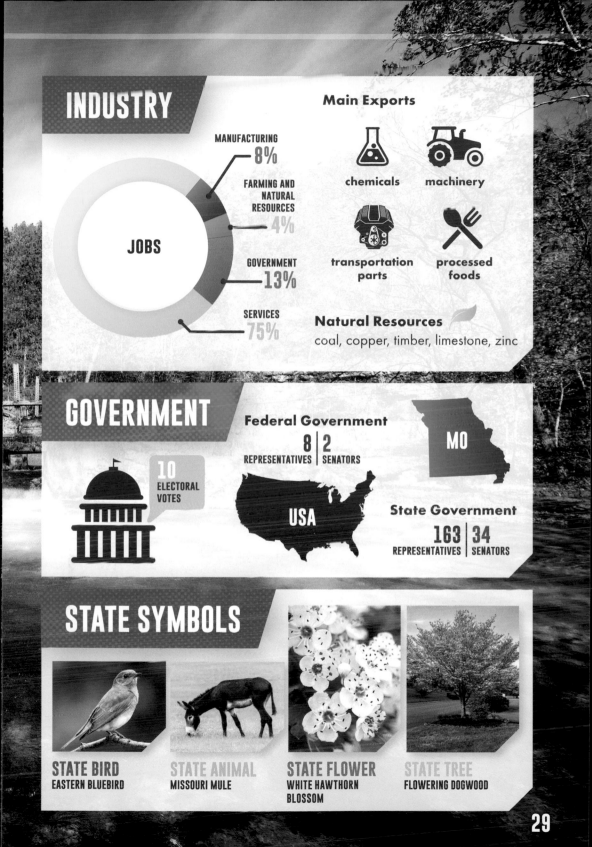

JOBS

MANUFACTURING
8%

FARMING AND
NATURAL
RESOURCES
4%

GOVERNMENT
13%

SERVICES
75%

chemicals

machinery

transportation parts

processed foods

Natural Resources
coal, copper, timber, limestone, zinc

GOVERNMENT

Federal Government

8 REPRESENTATIVES | **2** SENATORS

MO

10 ELECTORAL VOTES

USA

State Government

163 REPRESENTATIVES | **34** SENATORS

STATE SYMBOLS

STATE BIRD
EASTERN BLUEBIRD

STATE ANIMAL
MISSOURI MULE

STATE FLOWER
WHITE HAWTHORN BLOSSOM

STATE TREE
FLOWERING DOGWOOD

29

Civil War—a war between the Northern (Union) and Southern (Confederate) states that lasted from 1861 to 1865

cultural—relating to the beliefs, arts, and ways of life in a place or society

custard—a dish that is thickened with eggs

descent—background or ancestry

hub—a center of activity

immigrants—people who move to a new country

Louisiana Purchase—a deal made between France and the United States; it gave the United States 828,000 square miles (2,144,510 square kilometers) of land west of the Mississippi River.

manufacturing—a field of work in which people use machines to make products

Midwestern—related to a region of 12 states in the north-central United States

Missouri Compromise—an 1820 agreement that admitted Missouri into the United States as a slave state and Maine as a free state; the Missouri Compromise banned slavery in future states or territories north of Missouri's southern border.

natural resources—materials in the earth that are taken out and used to make products or fuel

plains—large areas of flat land

service jobs—jobs that perform tasks for people or businesses

settlers—people who move to live in a new, undeveloped region

urban—related to cities and city life

AT THE LIBRARY

Mattern, Joanne. *The Gateway Arch: Celebrating Western Expansion*. South Egremont, Mass.: Red Chair Press, 2018.

Murray, Julie. *Missouri*. Minneapolis, Minn.: Abdo Publishing, 2020.

Zeiger, Jennifer. *Missouri*. New York, N.Y.: Children's Press, 2019.

ON THE WEB

FACTSURFER

Factsurfer.com gives you a safe, fun way to find more information.

1. Go to www.factsurfer.com.

2. Enter "Missouri" into the search box and click $\mathcal{Q}$.

3. Select your book cover to see a list of related content.

INDEX